A REAL LIFE AMERICAN DREAM

The John H. McClatchy Story

Susan Marie Chapman

Printed in the United States of America

ISBN: 979 8 9922223 9 5

"I like to work while others are sleeping."
John Henry McClatchy

Table of Contents

For the McClatchy Clan

And to our President, Donald J. Trump, (a builder himself) for bringing back the American Dream.

Foreword

This true story is very personal to me because I am a great granddaughter to this magnificent pioneer. My grandmother was John H's daughter and my dad was his grandson. Growing up. I heard many stories about John H and his wife, May, and how they raised eleven children together. They build a home on the outskirts of the city of Philadelphia large enough to accommodate all of their children and 55 grandchildren with each child having their own set of rooms. Their home in New Jersey was built on an entire block in Ocean City that looked out to the ocean. It was so massive that people passing by often mistook it for a hotel and again, just like in Pennsylvania, each child had their own wing where they could stay with their families. My dad often talked about spending his summers in Ocean City, New Jersey with all of his cousins and the mischief they would get into. He also told me stories about his grandfather, waking up all the grandchildren very early in the morning at their beach house to go to New York City, to the Worlds Fair or to the museums. My dad described his grandfather as kind and wonderful, always smiling and laughing and never mean or cross. John H. McClatchy and his wife, May, both passed away in 1960, one month apart. I was two years old at the time.

CHAPTER 1

Childhood

Hi. My name is John Henry McClatchy, but all my friends call me John H., so I guess you can, too. As I think back on my long life now that I am passing seventy two years of age, I can reflect on the story of how I lived a real life American dream. It all started in Baltimore, Maryland on February 2, 1875, the day I was born.

My parents, George and Elizabeth McClatchy, had seven children and I was the eldest. My grandparents came to America as immigrants from Ireland and Scotland on my dad's side and Germany on my mom's side. I was eleven years old when my father decided to move us all to Philadelphia, Pennsylvania.

My parents never had $500 dollars at any time in their lives. In the year 1888, at the tender age of thirteen, I had to stop going to school and start working. I got a job in an office building at 5th and Chestnut Streets in the city of Philadelphia. I worked as an errand boy for a man named Clifford Pemberton Jr., who was a member of an old Philadelphia family and who had just started a building company. I stayed at this place, working for this man, and grew up with his business, which was a successful one.

**

Remember, this was the 1800s, and things were done a little bit different back then. Most cities were built next to a body of water, where boats could pick up and drop off goods and services and people traveling. Everything was done manually back then. We did not have UPS or Amazon. We didn't even have computers or phones. Sometimes it took several months or even a year for a package or letter to arrive at its destination.

My dad was a good, hard working man, but like a lot of men in the building trades at the time, he was out of work quite a bit. My family needed the money I brought home. The house we lived in cost $14 dollars a month, and the money I earned helped pay for that, but we always needed more. So I got an extra job carrying meat for a butcher. Every day, I started at 5:00 am in the morning, carrying the meat from the butcher shop to a small restaurant close to the Penrose Ferry Bridge. I carried the meat in a soapbox that sat on two old baby carriage wheels and steered with a stick in the front. I received $1.50 a week for this job.

**

After delivering the meat, I got home around 6:30 a.m., had my breakfast, then walked thirty five blocks to work in Mr. Pemberton's office, where I made $3 dollars a week in wages. I worked until 5:00 p.m., including Saturdays, and then I went straight to my third job. This was in the basement of a building on Third Street below Chestnut Street. My job was to carry scorecards from the basement office to cigar stores and saloons.

In those days, the latest evening newspapers were printed at 4 p.m. and the scorecards were printed at 5:45 p.m. The scorecards I delivered contained the latest baseball scores. I received another $1.50 a week for carrying the score cards around a planned route. Then, at around the same time, I got a fourth job, selling Sunday newspapers. I would leave my house at 3:30 a.m. — a little fellow fourteen years of age — and walk thirty five blocks through the dark, empty streets to get my bundle of Sunday newspapers to sell.

. **

I carried the newspapers over my shoulder with a big strap for ten more blocks, and then I would get on the dinky, one horse Toonerville car line that ran along Passyunk Avenue and arrive at the Catholic church just in time for the 6:00 a.m. Mass. After Mass, I would stand outside the church and sell papers as the people came out. When the church was empty, I would walk up one street after another shouting, "Here you are! Get your Sunday morning papers!"

The Sunday *Philadelphia Record* sold for two cents a copy, and the *Sunday Press*, which was the well known paper of that time, sold for four or five cents. After selling as many papers as I could, I would walk home to have breakfast around 9:30 a.m. Altogether I brought home $7 dollars a week to my parents, which was a lot of money back in those days. I knew from working with a butcher that you could buy three pounds of pork chops for twenty four cents and two pounds of beef steak for fifty cents.

**

Looking back, it is hard to believe I had such energy, but I kept working these four jobs and giving all my money to my parents until I was sixteen. That's when my father had a heart attack and died, and I became the man of the house. It was a very sad time in my family's life, and difficult, too.

My weekday became longer at this time. Instead of getting up at 5 a.m., I now got up at 3:30 a.m. to sell the daily newspaper before I went to my job at the butcher shop. I could not let my mother or my siblings down.

**

Now, let's skip to the year 1896. That is when I first met my wife to be, the most wonderful woman in the world. It was a very cold day in February, right around my birthday. I headed to the Schuylkill River to go ice skating, which was a favorite pastime for many Philadelphians in the 1800s. On this particular day, I noticed a young girl in the distance struggling to get her skates on. I offered my assistance, and we became fast friends. Mary Elizabeth Paradise, or "May," as she was affectionately called, was from Prince Edward Island in Canada. Our friendship quickly progressed towards a formal engagement.

***

CHAPTER 2

Family And Faith

May's parents had moved to Providence, Rhode Island, and then to Philadelphia when she was a young girl. As fate would have it, we met, and I always thought how lucky I was to be in that very spot at that moment in time. But at this stage in my life, I had nothing to offer my future wife. I didn't have a home, and I did not have the income to support a family. I decided to go to my boss, Mr. Clifford Pemberton Jr., with a proposal.

As you know, Pemberton was a builder/contractor. He had three houses that he couldn't sell. They had been sitting empty for a long time. I asked Mr. Pemberton whether, if I could sell those three homes at asking price and very quickly, would he be willing to give me a home for myself? My boss agreed. I sold the houses right away and at full price. I finally had a home for myself and my wife to be, and we quickly set a date to be married. I had found my calling. Building and selling homes was something I was really good at.

**

May and I were married the next year, in 1897, and we decided to start a family right away. We also agreed that I would go into business for myself in a very humble way. I felt confident that I could and would be very good at real estate, so in December of 1900, I started my own building company. I only had $25 dollars cash that I had saved up during my years of working for Mr. Pemberton. I started out by purchasing stationary, a desk, and a chair. The cost to do all of this was $10 dollars.

By that time, May and I already had three little children and some other serious family obligations. But my wife still found the time to write a large number of letters for me on the typewriter during the day while I was in town trying to drum up business. She was a tremendous help to me. I had married the most wonderful woman in the world. I always said, "Providence had provided me with a Paradise."

**

The first year we had our own business, May and I hoped to make $1,000 dollars. Instead, we made over $10,000 dollars, and the business kept on growing over the years. All of this was due to my wife, who was an inspiration to me every day of our very, very happily married life together.

I used to leave the house at six in the morning and not arrive home again until well into the evening. After about seven years of long hours and hard work, we were able to buy land on the outskirts of the city. It was there that we built our new home, with a large stable for our horses with living quarters overhead and a driveway and plantings. We also bought land in Ocean City, New Jersey, where we built a very large shore house on the beach. The cost of all of this was nearly $150,000, which included the rugs and furnishings. It was all paid for with a mortgage of $10,000.

**

I used to say that I was going to retire when I got to be worth $50,000, but instead I kept on going. I made large sums of money and carried over $1 million dollars of life insurance in addition to accident insurance and health insurance for my family's protection. I had to cash in most of this insurance during the Great Financial Crash in 1929, a situation that persisted through 1933, when all of the banks and trust companies in the entire United States closed down. The value of nearly everything collapsed. I had a lot of financial headaches at this time because everybody had them when all the banks closed. But I just took it all in my stride because I tried to be a regular guy. I will say more about this great panic and crash and its effect on my business and family later.

**

CHAPTER 3

The Great American Dream

In 1916, I developed land that I purchased outside of the city of Philadelphia. I built duplexes made out of stone, with slate roofs and hardwood floors. These sold for prices between $4,300 and $6,000.

I often sold these homes the same day I announced a new street was going up. The wood came from a lumber mill that I owned in Chester County, Pennsylvania. The stone came from my quarry from the same area. I also built an on site blacksmith shop where I was working to make sure that my two hundred workhorses were well taken care of and shod.

By the year 1918, May and I had thirteen children, but two of our baby boys died in childbirth. We were brokenhearted. It was a very sad time in our lives. We loved all of our children, including the ones in heaven. May had her hands full with all the responsibilities at home, and well, I just kept working.

***

Development after development followed, and then, in the early 1920s, I bought another piece of farmland located on Market Street and 69th Street on the outskirts of Philadelphia. This farmland would later become the 69th Street Boulevard shopping area.

The only way to describe it is to say that it was a continuous strip of stores on both sides of the street. It was my creation and concept. I had a vision and big dreams. The fact that 69th Street sat on a hill was a big challenge. I had to lower the ground by eight feet and then level it so that we could pave the road. I did this by using one hundred dump wagons, two hundred horses, and a crew of men with shovels and picks and baskets. Nothing is impossible if you can believe in it.

I built my four story office building called, The McClatchy Building, as the cornerstone of the 69th Street Boulevard. Today it is a historical site in Philadelphia. I planned and pushed hard for a million dollar parking lot called "The Parketeria," which opened in October of 1928. It was free parking for more than four thousand motorists a day and it was full every day.

***

I also provided a daycare for the children of the shoppers so that mothers and fathers could drop off their little ones to be entertained by shows like *Punch and Judy* while their parents shopped. This was another first, and an idea that was ahead of its time.

My eldest son, John B., joined the business at this time and was a great asset to me. He deserves credit for getting the great stores to come to the 69th Street Boulevard. Let me explain this a little better. We owned all of the buildings, and the stores that came here rented from us. I was the first commercial realtor in the world to offer leases that started out low and increased as the store's sales increased. Instead of charging each store a fixed rent, I asked for 2 percent of the gross sales. This way I could be more like a partner than a landlord, committed to the financial success of each retail establishment.

**

Some of the stores that we invited to come and be a part of 69th Street Boulevard were the big A&P grocery store, Penn Fruit Company, and Woolworth's five and ten store. We also had the Whelan's Drug Store, Lords Store, Lit Brothers, Gimbels, Horn & Hardhardt, and many shoe stores like Lanes and Reids, and Helen Caro. Prior to the grand opening in 1928, I took out full page ads in the Philadelphia newspapers, including the *Evening Bulletin*, the *Inquirer*, the *Record*, and the *Public Ledger*.

My third oldest son, Richard A. McClatchy, who is about nine years younger than John B., also came into the business at this time. His work was always more in the house building side of things and not in the planning of the stores. Both sons were great assets to me and my businesses.

***

On the day of the opening of the 69th Street Boulevard, there were parades with marching bands, and a crowd of nearly four hundred thousand people. Visitors thronged the streets from sidewalk to sidewalk. The streets had to be closed to all vehicles. It was quite spectacular.

I have often been asked about my work routine and it's quite simple. I am up early every morning and get to church in time for the 6:30 am Mass. Afterwards, I head to the office, arriving before 8 a.m. This routine still stands to this day, even after retiring. As I always say, "I like to work while others are sleeping."

**

In 1927, my income was $27 million for that year alone, and I had to pay taxes on all of it. I paid $7 million in taxes, (the highest of anyone in the entire United States for that year)—such an enormous amount that I was invited to the nation's capital by the Secretary of the Treasury, Andrew Mellon, to meet with President Calvin Coolidge. They wanted to talk to me about tax shelters and write offs. "What a privilege it was to meet our president," I thought as I rode the train back from Washington D.C.

***

CHAPTER 4

The Great Financial Crisis

Right in the middle of building and getting all these fine stores to come to 69th Street, the Great Financial Crisis happened. It started in October of 1929 and was the greatest economic downturn that had occurred in the experience of any living man. Large businesses and firms, hundreds of building and loan associations, banks, trust companies, and savings fund societies went into bankruptcy. They were closing their doors every day and nothing seemed to have any value.

In my own line of business, it was chaos. Foreclosures happened on the first Monday of every month, and in one month, two thousand, two hundred and twenty two properties were sold at a sheriff's sale. This continued every month for over a year. To put it in perspective, one block generally contains about thirty homes, so this was about seventy three blocks of homes being sold at one time. Imagine so many family homes, all selling at foreclosure rates in a single month.

***

Unfortunately, the massive sell off of homes lasted far longer than one month. In one year, nearly twenty five thousand and two hundred homes were sold off at auction. Just think a little, just picture yourself walking past or along one side of the street of houses in the city, one block long. Then keep walking and walking until you walked over eight hundred city blocks and then you would get an impression you would never, never forget, remembering that all these houses were sold at sheriff sale in practically one year. This figure was for the city of Philadelphia alone, and did not include neighboring counties.

Stop and reflect on this, on the enormous scale of financial ruin. It will possibly show you what a great crisis this was and make you wonder how I was not swallowed up in this great collapse, which certainly engulfed most Americans.

***

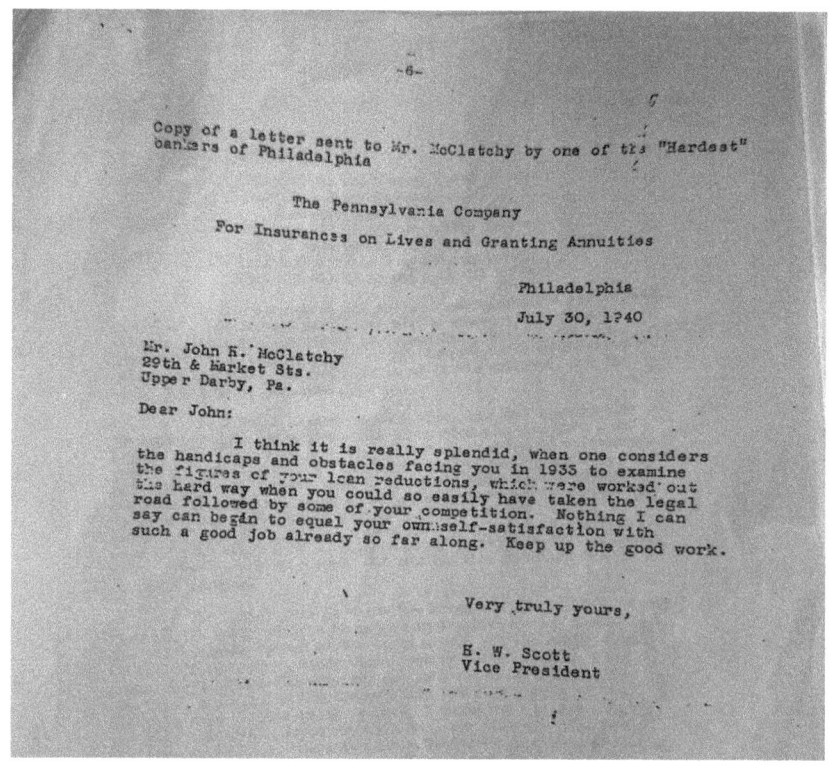

Letter sent to John H. from H.W. Scott vp of Pennsylvania Bank Co.

John H. McClatchy early 1900.

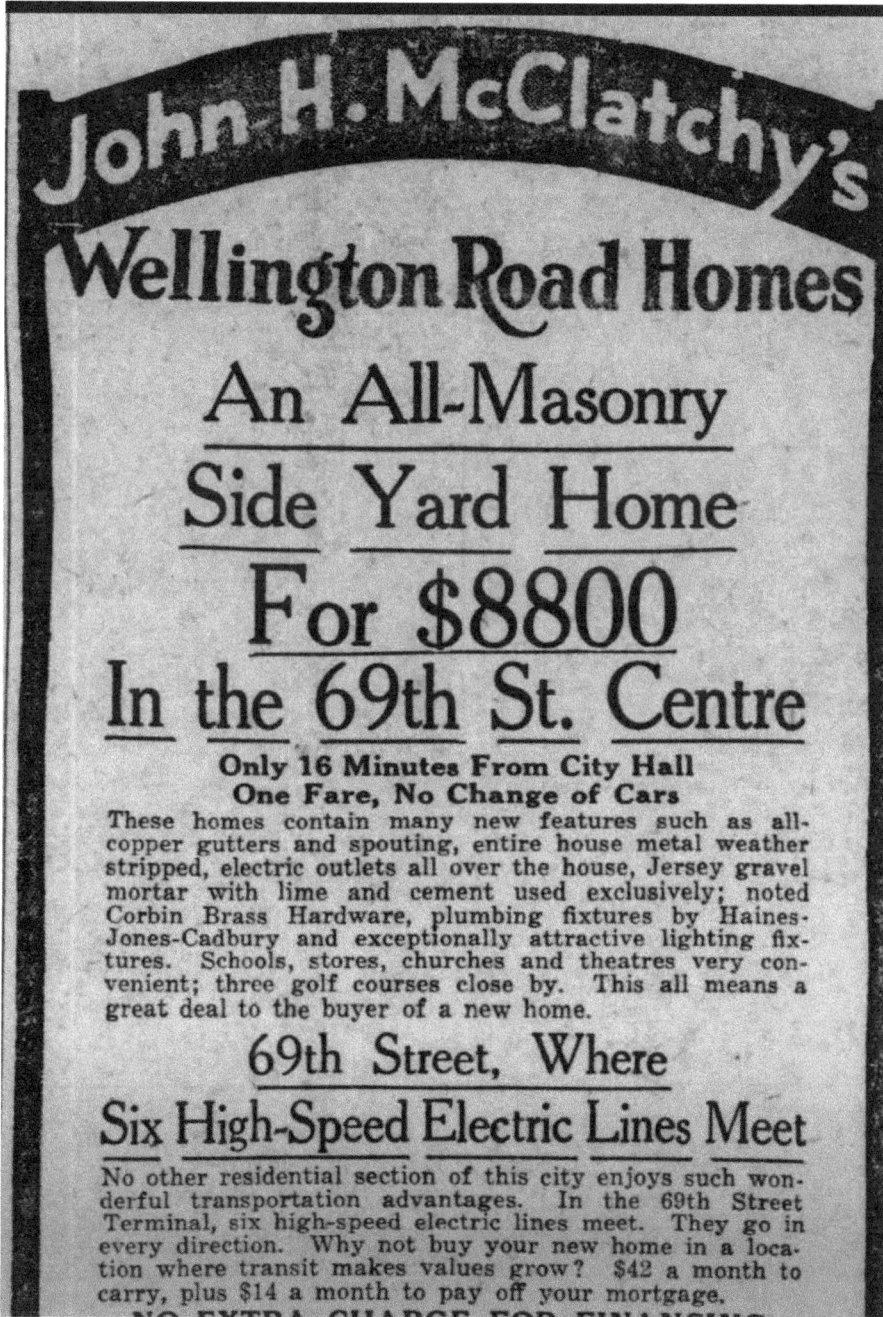

John H McClatchy 80 years old, 1955.

Easter bunny 69th Street Blvd.

Old architectual plans for 69th Street Blvd.

Punch and Judy Puppet Show.

Frank A. McClatchy was mistaken for his brother John H.
and kidnapped and murdered by gangsters

Historical Philadelphia 1920s.

Philadelphia 1920s.

McClatchy building 69th Street Blvd.

McClatchty family portrait, 1920s

Mary Elizabeth Paradise.

Finally, in 1933, the United States government ordered all banks and trust companies in the country to close their doors. Imagine what that was like! A dear friend of mine, William Friehofer, who was president of the Friehofer Banking Company, went bankrupt. He was also the president of the Trust Company, and that went bankrupt, too.

Hundreds and hundreds of people whose life savings were in Friehofer's bank stormed the doors, demanding to get some of their hard earned money back. I had large investments in vacant land in the 69th Street area and elsewhere and had borrowed large sums of money on mortgage loans. Some of the banks I had borrowed from were in serious financial trouble, and demanded that I pay off all, or at least part, of my loans.

In order to find a solution to the situation, I asked all of the trust companies, banks, insurance companies, and savings fund societies that I did business with to meet with me. We had a very memorable meeting, gathered around a table at the office of one of the largest banks in the state of Pennsylvania.

***

My son, John B., was there with me and as a result of this meeting, the bankers appointed a committee to take charge of my affairs. I agreed to work with them to straighten everything out and they all agreed to give me time to do this. But no definite length of time to sort things out was established, and I was well aware that the loans could be called in at any moment, which would put all of my businesses in serious jeopardy.

This was not a very good arrangement for me, but it was the best I could do at the time, and I trusted that even though they also didn't know what to expect, the banks would show me every consideration and do the best they could. But, as I stated, some of these banks and trust companies had serious troubles of their own, making it a very scary time for all. The very reminder of this makes me shudder, even now.

***

This was a very stressful time for me and for my family, but what kept me going was the love of my wife and my eleven children. We would often leave Philadelphia and travel to our house in Ocean City, New Jersey. I wanted to say a little bit more about my shore home. It was a very large house, and it was built so that each one of my children had their own set of rooms, almost like an apartment for each family. This house was built on a whole block of land and was very large. It almost looked like a hotel. During our times at the shore, I loved to drive my little children around in a buckboard or watch as they rode their ponies on the beach. There was a small stable down the street from where we lived, and I purchased the stable and all the ponies and equipment so that my children could ride the ponies every day if they wished. My biggest success in life was my family, and relaxing for me was spending time at home. I did not drink alcohol, nor did I gamble or smoke, and I never considered doing those things. I found all of my joy in my family and in God.

After my children came into their teens, I would stay up every night until the last one came home. As the years went by, my wife and I watched as our forty six grandchildren and sixty great grandchildren arrived. I delighted in taking a bunch of them to an automat and watching as they raced about, each with a handful of nickels, shouting and pulling levers for their food and beverages. Sometimes I would wake them up very early in the morning, before it was light out, and tell them to get dressed because I was taking them to the World's Fair or the Metropolitan Museum. I loved New York City and all that it had to offer, and I wanted my grandchildren to experience it, too.

***

On July 23,1933, wealth brought tragedy to our family when my younger brother, Frank, a real estate agent, was lured by gangsters to a housing development just outside the city limits. He resisted the gangsters' efforts to kidnap him and was shot in the stomach. He died a short time later at the Misericordia Hospital. I believe that I was their intended target and when they realized they had the wrong McClatchy, they shot Frank and left him for dead. This affected me deeply. Frank was a good man and my brother, and I loved him.

***

Throughout the Great Financial Crisis, I kept fighting to protect my whole family: my children and their spouses, and my grandchildren and great grandchildren. My son John B. was by my side through the fight.

We made various efforts to get aid to help keep our businesses afloat, working day and night. We had a bankruptcy petition made up and ready to file at any time if any one of the lending companies tried to take advantage of us. But despite our many meetings, some of which extended far into the night, all of these efforts failed. After many consultations, George K. Watson of George K. Watson & Co., who was appointed by the banking committee to go over our books, advised me to go into bankruptcy.

***

Effingham B. Morris, president of one of the largest trust companies, Girard Trust, had known me from boyhood and had always been very kind to me. He finally advised me to go into bankruptcy, too, and a statement of bankruptcy was finally prepared.

So many men I knew and had done business with had gone into bankruptcy at some point. They took this action to wipe out all their troubles and worries and get a new clean start. John B. and I had always been opposed to this action. I told Mr. Morris and others that hardly any other man in business facing bankruptcy had as much at stake as I had: namely, the effect on the future of my unusually large family of children and grandchildren.

Though I was advised to declare bankruptcy, I could never bring myself to do it. Letters like the one I received from H.W. Scott of the Pennsylvania Company reminded me that my decision was the correct one.

***

CHAPTER 5

Reflection and Gratitude

I have been at the office very little during these last few months. I have been spending my time at my son, Paul's farm, leaving the house around 7:00 a.m. and not returning until 6:30 pm. I have also been attending farm sales and the popular weekly cattle sales at Ephrata, New Holland, and Belleville in Lancaster County, Pennsylvania.

It was all quite interesting and caused me to meet a different class of people than I had ever met in my sixty years of real estate business and construction. I was in the company of farmers, dairy farmers, cattle dealers, and the presidents of banks that were also farmers. I met with beef and pork and calf buyers, Amish people, Mennonites, and thrifty Pennsylvania Dutch people.

***

I made an effort to discuss family and business matters with the farmers that I was meeting. Not all would loosen up at first. But, by telling them about my big family and business experiences and by showing them the picture of the fifty four members of our family taken at the celebration of my fiftieth wedding anniversary with May, some of them softened up a little bit and talked quite freely. For the most part though, it was very interesting and also instructive. I learned about the simple way of life from some. It was a way of life growing crops, harvesting, milking cows, feeding your family and getting up at the crack of dawn and not leaving the work until darkness made you stop.

Since Lancaster County is quite a distance from the city of Philadelphia, these trips gave me plenty of time for reflection. I thought a lot about the hectic life I had led and the large amounts of money I had borrowed during my long years in business. Each new business venture was full of risk. I have also seen failures of all kinds, not just in business, but also moral failures in the men around me. Some of them ended in suicide.

***

The contrast between the simple lives of these farmers and the nerve wracking big business life that I had lived made me think a lot, and I often reflected on the folly of it all. How did I get into this crazy life that I have lived? Let us review the matter together, children and grandchildren and great grandchildren, sons in law, daughters in law. Let us all study it.

John H. McClatchy never declared bankruptcy, and his career continued long after the financial crisis had passed. On the occasion of his 80th birthday, which coincided with the 25th anniversary of the 69th Street shopping area, he was interviewed by the newspaper about his long career. "It was in the year 1900 that I decided to start my own business. At that time I had about $15 and three children." He remarked that there had been a point at which he'd considered retirement, but "the children kept coming and dreams of further development wouldn't stop."

John H. McClatchy never sought to speak about himself, but by all accounts, his impact on the Philadelphia area was profound. In an article from January of 1947 titled, "When Something Happens to John H. McClatchy, It's News in Upper Darby," the reporter wrote:

Although his formal schooling ended at twelve, Mr. McClatchy today is rated one of the foremost authorities on business and real estate law in eastern Pennsylvania. A photographic memory and alert mind and a vast capacity for work leaves his associates agape even today. Despite the fact that his sons have taken over the burden of much of the office responsibilities, Mr. John H. McClatchy still shows up for work every day in the week before most offices in his building are open. He knows the name of every grandchild (48), a feat in itself, and maintains an infallible grasp over every detail of his enterprises. Most surprised man in Upper Darby when this piece appears will be Mr. McClatchy. For a lifetime he has shied away from publicity, will never pose for a picture, never talk for publications and he wouldn't talk now. Reporters pieced this together from friends who insisted his story needed to be told.

***

After his death, John H. McClatchy was inducted into the Home Builders Hall of Fame on December 2, 1960. In a write up about this honor, it was noted that "John H. was one of the great American builders of the century and the entire 69th Street area in Upper Darby is a monument to his genius as a builder and developer. McClatchy also was one of the founders of the Home Builders Association of Philadelphia and suburban counties which sponsors the Hall of Fame. His name appears on the original charter."

Furthermore, at a June meeting of the Board of Directors of the Delaware County Real Estate Board, a declaration was passed in his honor: "Be it resolved that the passing of John H. McClatchy, affectionately known to all Board members as 'John H.,' has been noted with regret and sorrow. The fact that he built over 40,000 homes and developed 69th Street Boulevard into a nationally famous shopping center is over-shadowed by the inspiring family, charitable and religious life which he quietly led."

***

John H. McClatchy passed away on March 12, 1960. He was 85 years old and died a very wealthy man. His wife May passed away exactly one month before him, on February 11, 1960. John and May had been married for sixty three years, had thirteen children, forty eight grandchildren, and sixty great grandchildren. John H. knew every one of them by name.

After his passing, John H. was mourned and remembered by many. As one local newspaper wrote, "We remember a tall, stooped man, striding confidently across the street he created. A kindly gentleman with a courtly manor, and an old world courtesy. A man who knew how to be right, fully proud of his accomplishments, without arrogance or smugness. The legend built around this remarkable man fits perfectly into the picture of John H. McClatchy, as we remember him personally during those last years in which he played an active role in the real estate empire he founded."

In an article by Jane Galloway in March of 1994 titled, "69th Street Was Where to See the Easter Bunny," Dr. Stephen T. Whelan an Upper Darby dermatologist and the voice of the Easter Bunny that stood at the top of the 69th Street hill for over 35 years, recalled John H. McClatchy, whom he knew well. Whelan's parents had been among the very first residents to buy a McClatchy home. "He was an impressive man," says Whelan. "He was always very positive about what he was going to do and forceful in speaking about it. McClatchy was a big man. He was over 6 feet tall, with blue eyes and dark hair and he always wore a business suit."

Bibliography

Bjorkgven, David, ed. "Thousands in Final Tribute to John McClatchy." *The News of Delaware County,*

March 18, 2011, sec. Yesterday's Papers: Facts & Fancies.

"Downtown Upper Darby Vision Plan." Delaware County PA, May 2018. https://www.delcopa.gov/planning/pubs/DowntownUpperDarbyVisionPlan.pdf.

Everts, Bart. "Have Art, Will Travel: Uncovering the 69th Street Branch of PMA." Hidden City Philadelphia, January 31, 2020. https://hiddencityphila.org/2020/01/have art will travel uncovering the 69th street branch of pma/.

Herr Cardillo, Starr. "Art Deco Enclave in Upper Darby a Display for the Ages." Hidden City Philadelphia,

February 7, 2018. https://hiddencityphila.org/2018/02/art deco enclave in upper darby a display for the ages/.

Huff, Minne N. "Proud 'Mr John H.' at 80 Surveys 69th Street His Miracle Avenue of Dreams," February 13, 1953.

"John H. McClatchy, Builder, Developer, Is Dead at Age 85."

Philadelphia Inquirer, March 13, 1960.

"John H. McClatchys Celebrate Golden Wedding Saturday with 10 Children, 38 Grandchildren Present at

Observance." *Delaware County Daily Times*, January 23, 1947.

McClatchy, John H. 1947. *The Journals of John H. McClatchy.*

Scott, H.W. Letter to John H. McClatchy. Philadelphia, Pennsylvania, July 30, 1940.

"When Something Happens to John H. McClatchy, It's News in Upper Darby." *The News of Delaware County*, January 23, 1947.